The Mindfulness of Italy

By Dr. Jo-Ann Petrucci Andrews

Photography by Benjamin Conroy Andrews

Stillwater River

The Mindfulness of Italy Copyright © 2017 Jo-Ann Petrucci Andrews. Produced and printed by Stillwater River Publications. All rights reserved. Written and produced in the United States of America. This book may not be reproduced or sold in any form without the expressed, written permission of the au-thors and publisher.

Visit our website at **www.StillwaterPress.com** for more information.

First Stillwater River Publications Edition

ISBN-10: 1-946-30011-X
ISBN-13: 978-1-946300-11-9

Library of Congress Control Number: 2017941951

1 2 3 4 5 6 7 8 9 10
Written by Jo-Ann Petrucci-Andrews
Photographs by Benjamin Conroy Andrews
Published by Stillwater River Publications, Glocester, RI, USA.

Proceeds from the sale of this book will be donated to Miracle Books, a non-profit organization. Miracle Books is organized exclusively for charitable, religious, educational, and scientific purposes, including for such purposes, the making of distributions to organizations that qualify as exempt organizations under section 501(c)(3) of the Internal Revenue Code, or the corresponding section of any future federal tax code.

The views and opinions expressed in this book are solely those of the author and do not necessarily reflect the views and opinions of the publisher.

This book is not intended as a substitute for the medical advice of physicians. The reader should regularly consult a physician in matters relating to his/her health and particularly with respect to any symptoms that may require diagnosis or medical attention.

Thanks to
Father Derpich Nikola
My brother-in-law, Craig Berntson for his help
proofing the book
As well as all of the Intermezzo Travelers
Caroline Pugsley

Life is a journey no matter how far you travel.

Dedication

To my loving husband, Ben.

Father Derpich Nikola.

A special thanks to my mom,
Vicenza Jennie Colantonio Petrucci

In honor of my northern Italian
Grandmother and Grandfather Colantonio
and Grandmother and Grandfather Petrucci.

And to my family and friends
who supported me on this journey.

Antioxidants

Antioxidants help stabilize the body. Eat foods that contain antioxidant vitamins, such as A, B, C, D and E. These vitamins help boost the immune system as well as fight infections and diseases. Italy has many foods that are rich in antioxidants and polyphenols, such as olive oil which contains polyphenols and Vitamin E. There are many health benefits to eating foods that absorb free radicals and appear to have a positive impact on our health. They also appear to have a helpful impact on cardiovascular and cancer ailments, as suggested by the region's Mediterranean diet.

Palazzo Barbieri, Verona

Centro Storico, Verona

B

B Vitamins

B vitamins -- B1, B2, B3, B5, B6, B7, B9, B12 -- are filled with nutritional value and can help prevent strokes. They are also of value for skin, hair and better metabolism. Referred to as vitamin B complex, B vitamins play an important role in keeping bodies fit. They are the essential nutrients that help convert our food into fuel, which allows us to stay energized throughout the day. While many of the following vitamins work in tandem, each has its own specific benefits – from promoting healthy skin and hair to preventing memory loss and migraines. There is a rich variety of B Vitamins found in the foods in Italy. B1, B2, B6, B12, and calcium pantothenate are found in Italian cheese such as parmigiano-Reggiano, pecorino, Romano and gorgonzola.

San Marco, Venice

Dorsoduro, Venice

C

Care for Yourself

Take time to exercise, eat nutritional food, and treat your body with the care it deserves. Italians eat a Mediterranean diet. This includes a lot of fresh fish, fruit, vegetables, nuts, seeds and olive oil. And there is mounting evidence that such a diet can significantly prolong life and reduce the risk of heart disease and cancer.

Each journey starts with the first step…

There is a Celtic proverb that says, *"To understand where you are going you must understand where you came from."*

This is the beginning of a new chapter for me -- leaving the United Sates for Italy. What an adventure! How exciting! The flight attendant is preparing the passengers for takeoff, and the first item on her agenda is the oxygen mask. In case of an emergency, please apply your oxygen mask to yourself before giving the mask to the person beside you.

The reason is that our inclination is to take care of the people we love and care about first: children, sisters, spouses, and friends. But if we give all of ourselves, depleting our self of oxygen, how can we help anyone else? The well-known rock musician and singer Janis Joplin once said, "Don't compromise yourself. You're all you've got." My experience is that we can become very bitter if we keep giving and giving yet neglect ourselves. At the end of the day, it's nobody's fault but our own for not taking care of us.

☼☼☼

"Make the most of yourself, for that is all there is of you."
                                         -- Ralph Waldo Emerson

D
Diet

Enjoy *la dolce vita* (the good life)!

Italy is known for its great food, yet their obesity rate is really low compared with the other countries in Europe and the United States. Diet is essential to overall health. "Italians don't get fat" is a popular saying to describe Italian food and lifestyle.

Vitamin D -- get your Vitamin D level checked. Low Vitamin D levels can lead to major medical and psychiatric issues. Low vitamin D can also be the culprit to depression, in particular, seasonal affective disorder (SAD).

Colloquium, Ice Skating in Rome, Roma, Colosseo

Vatican, Rome - Roma, Vaticano, Ponte

E
Exercise

Try to exercise every day. If you can't, then at least try to find an opportunity to walk even if it means you must park your car further away to have the chance to take more steps. In Italy, 28 percent of journeys are made on foot compared with 12 percent in the U.S. And then there's the fact that Italians famously take a walk -- a *passeggiata* -- after dinner. Remember to live an active lifestyle as this will increase both mental and physical longevity.

"Gratitude turns what we have into enough."

Research shows that optimism and trying to remain positive can boost the immune system, decrease infection, and warn-off chronic disease such as cancer. Although easier said than done, there are ways to support positivity and an optimistic mindset. We tend to forget that happiness doesn't come as a result of getting something we don't have, but rather from recognizing and appreciating what we do have.

Gratitude associated with optimism is the ability to be grateful for all things and to appreciate the value of what is around us. And that includes the people in our lives. Gratitude turns what we have into enough.

✵✵✵

"Go confidently in the direction of your dreams. Live the life You have imagined."

–Henry David Thoreau

F

Family

Famiglia (Latin: familia) is a group of people either joined by birth or by co-residence. However you define your family, remember to put work into this relationship as it is the most significant of socialization.

Socialization and interaction in the world promotes positive mental health and longevity. Italians place a great emphasis on family. Everywhere you go in Italy, families gather and communicate with language face to face, and rarely carry electronic devices when together. Remember: food, family, and friends are important in your daily life. Whoever you define as your family, remember to make time every day to communicate and engage with them.

Aperto Restaurant, Rome - Sant'Eustachio

Bernini Ristorante-Pizzeria, Rome: Celio, Navona, Monti, Pigna

G

Go Outdoors

Be active in the outdoors every day. Whether it is hiking, sailing, biking, soccer, or even climbing a volcano, try to be as active as you can. Italians are very active, always moving, and never depending on transportation, but relying on their own energy to take them back and forth.

Be on the lookout for beauty everywhere.

Mindfulness is having the ability for acceptance, mainly, acceptance of self.

Mindfulness is being present in the moment while also being aware of your thoughts and feelings. However, mindfulness includes understanding that our thoughts and feelings do not define who we are as human beings.

Coming to Italy was a dream come true. Learning about the great history and being a part of a privileged pilgrimage emerged while learning about the unfolding woven tapestry of rich culture. Italy is an ancient country with a vast history spanning thousands of years.

To stand and view sights of untold wonder and to walk in the footsteps of great conquerors, poets, artists, kings, queens and royalty, as well as biblical characters and martyrs, is almost surreal.

☼☼☼

"Everything has its beauty, but not everyone sees it."
-Confucius

H

Happiness

Don't be afraid to ask for help.

True happiness requires some measure of self-awareness. The best moments in our lives are not the passive, relaxing times, but the times when we accomplish something difficult and worthwhile. The Italians enjoy life, build social networks, and find community as an everyday important concept of life. The Italians say, *"La vera felicità richiede una certa dose di consapevolezza di sé."*

Many people find it difficult to relax their mind and find peace. Say these words out loud or to yourself: "May you live with ease. May you be happy. May you be free from pain." Remember to find happiness every day.

Ristorante pizzeria - Milan

Tuscany, Ristorante

I

Imagination

Sono tutte fantasie! -- It's all imagination! Imagination is essential for growth and development. When children are small, it is important that they are curious and explore their environment. A good imagination, curiosity, and exploration are good characteristics in an individual. No other country sees life the way Italy sees life. The Italian imagination has changed the world -- from ancient Rome, to the era of the big explorers, to the Renaissance, to the rise of the Catholic Church, and to modern times. Anyone who has had an opportunity to see the Vatican museums will see the works of the genius Michelangelo; his imagination had no boundaries. There is practically no area of life where the Italians haven't injected the vitality that characterizes them. Look at life and imagine what the possibilities could be!

I encourage my patients to write in a journal where they can process their feelings and emotions, particularly any feelings that they don't want to share with the world. There are many people who only see the negative -- no light, only darkness. Many people will look at a situation or see themselves with a negative eye. For this population, I highly recommend they create a "Thankful Journal." We need to look around us, no matter how bad it is, and see something good in it. Robert Louis Stevenson once said, "Don't judge each day by the harvest you reap but by the seeds that you plant."

Everything that happens to you is your teacher. 'The secret is to sit at the feet of your own life and be taught by it.
                                              -Mahatma Gandhi

J
Jazz

Jazz is a musical genre that enjoys a common bond among European and American cultures. Music can play a huge part in our feelings and behavior. Italy has always had a strong affinity for jazz. I noted that the jazz scene is particularly important in Milan and Rome. Italy is also a country that attracts many distinguished jazz musicians from all over the world.

Music is an important aspect of life, happiness, and ongoing pleasure, as many cultures have contributed their own experience and styles to the art form as well. Take time to let music be a part of your life, no matter which genre you prefer.

St. Francis of Assisi

K
Vitamin K

Vitamin K is known as a blood clotting vitamin. It assists in healing wounds. But it is important to know that Vitamin K works with calcium to improve bone functioning, too. Here is a list of foods that contain Vitamin K: green leafy vegetables, collards, green leaf lettuce, romaine lettuce, kale, mustard greens, parsley, spinach, broccoli, Brussels sprouts, cauliflower and cabbage.

Italy has many foods rich in vitamin K. An example would be the Romanesco broccoli, also known as Roman cauliflower, Broccolo Romanesco, Romanesque cauliflower or simply Romanesco. Romanesco is an edible flower (the species Brassica Oleracea) that was first documented in Italy. The Romanesco stems share the same toxic substances as rhubarb leaves, including oxalic acid, which is a nephrotoxic and corrosive acid that is present in many plants. It has been grown in Italy since the 16th Century. Food can be medicinal. Eat foods rich in K vitamins daily.

Ristorante Dorando, Assisi

Chapel of St. Francis of Assisi

L

Laugh

Living La dolce vita -- live a healthy life!

Laughter can not only feel good but it can also improve overall health. Laughter strengthens your immune system, boosts mood, can eliminate pain, and protects you from the damaging effects of stress. Everywhere you go in Italy, you find people gathering and laughing. Find an opportunity for laughter and improve your emotional health and happiness. The Italians believe in community, and this community adds to the quality of life.

Live in the present.

One of the take away memories from my trip to Italy is the slower pace. One of the ways we were able to make it back to the bus when going to a restaurant was to ask if they could make it American time. Italian time would mean hours waiting for our food. They are so much more relaxed and calm. We, as a society, are moving so quickly through life that we never have time not to be worried about time. Even when we are engaging in social activities such as dining out, we are still worried about making it somewhere else. Take time to take bliss in the moment, get pleasure from the food, and savor its flavor. Enjoy spending time with the people you're with. Get to know them, and most of all, find eternity in every moment.

Remaining positive about yourself and your situation can be difficult when things look bleak, but it is essential to stay positive for overall mental health and happiness. When stressors come a knockin', it's easy to throw in the towel and give up. But it's important to try to remain positive during these times because the negative attitude will enhance the situation and it will become even worse. Norman Vincent Peale once said, "Change your thoughts and you can change the world."

☼☼☼

The most important things in life are not things.

-Anonymous

Mindfulness

Mindfulness is the ability to be present in the moment. Italy's time, in comparison to America's time, is so much more relaxed. Sitting down for meals is a culinary experience not only because the food is amazing, but because the environment is so much more slow-paced. Meditation has a positive effect on well-being. Take time to meditate every day. Meditation can reduce negative emotions, reduce high blood pressure, and increase happiness overall. Live in the present. Live life with full intention and appreciate every moment.

Tuscany Hillside

N
Negativity

Be optimistic. Have the ability, with buoyancy and enthusiasm, to see the world as a good place. We went on several tours throughout Italy. Although each guide had their own style, they all ended the tour with a positive spin, joining us together as one people although we come from various parts of the world.

Great things are happening in your midst, but you need to look for them.

Try your best not to judge others, as we never truly know the road others walk upon. By judging others, we limit the opportunity to get to know someone for who that person really is, rather than by the way we think they are. The comedian Milton Berle once said, "If the opportunity doesn't knock, build a door."

"The less you open your heart to others, the more your heart suffers."

-Deepak Chopra

"The real voyage of discovery consists not in seeking new landscapes but in having new eye."

-Marcel Proust

O
Omega 3

Italy is a Mediterranean country where obesity is rare despite a profusion of pizza, pasta, and many other delicious foods. Omega 3 is found in fish including salmon, tuna, and anchovies. Many studies have found that a Mediterranean diet has numerous health benefits, from reducing the risk of cancer and heart disease to living a healthier, longer life. People who eat foods with high levels of Omega 3 have lower levels of depression and other mental health disorders. Additionally, Omega 3 appears to improve cognition and process associated with memory including executive functioning.

Grand Canal - Venice

Milan – Stanzione Centrale Est

P

Positive

Positivism is the ability to see the good in the world. Try your best to be a positive person. One of the tour guides at St Francis of Assisi ended our tour by saying, "we hear all bad news about people doing bad things, but in reality, people are mainly good. Let's focus on the good in the world instead of the bad."

San Gimignano

Quality

Quality of life matters! Let's face it, it's not just about "living," it's about the quality of life that counts. As we age, we are susceptible to a variety of age related issues, including cognitive and physical breakdown. Cell damage is the biggest culprit in the aging process, thus keeping cells healthy is essential to good health as well as slowing down the aging process. Italy ranks above average in quality of life, and in work, social connection, health, and balance. Italy measures very well in comparison to other countries.

Magic happens every day, we need to see it.

Don't listen to the negative voices inside your head. Theodore Roosevelt once said, "Do what you can, with what you have, where you are." Don't sabotage your own happiness and success by focusing in on the negative whispers that you hear. Don't allow self-defeat to conquer you; take control and conquer it! Focus on the positive aspects of yourself; build yourself up with positive words. Let the voices inside of you tell you words that feed you with nourishment.

Ralph Waldo Emerson once said, "What lies behind us and what lies before us are tiny matters compared to what lies within us. We have so much more potential than we give ourselves credit for. Be yourself, be unique, find your own pathway wherever it is and what ever direction the road takes you.

☼☼☼

"Do not go where the path may lead; go instead where there is no path and leave a trail."

-Ralph Waldo Emerson

R

Rest

The idea of mindfulness is really about pausing. Culturally speaking, the Italian culture definitely moves at a slower pace than the American culture. In Italy, there are "pausa," or midday breaks, where everything shuts down in the middle of the day for three to four hours. This is a time for relaxation, to eat a leisurely lunch, or to make time to socialize with others. We in American society have a lot to learn from this culture. So keep calm and carry on.

Florence in the afternoon

Florence in the morning

Sleep

Good sleep is essential for overall mental and physical health.

I have noted a high percentage of my patients complaining about insomnia and other sleep related issues. Italians take sleep and relaxation seriously. Interesting enough, there are studies that link irregular sleep schedules to the American adolescent population; however, there is evident to suggest that Italian adolescents reported much better sleep hygiene than U.S teens. Some interesting differences in sleep habits are probably culturally determined. I tell my patients to stay off electronic devices an hour or so before bed. Good sleep hygiene practices can result in a good night's sleep and lead to better cognitive processing and overall mental and physical health the next day.

Take time every day to meditate.

When life gets too hard to stand, then kneel and pray. When we place it out of our hands and release it -- letting it go into the universe -- we learn we can send that energy force away from us. This can often be our fears represented by anxiety that results in stress. Your hands are only so big, and our ability to think we can control the universe is unlimited. The search for meaning, questioning our life, is a constant battle we will never win and never be able to find peace. Take care of yourself; give yourself the oxygen mask. Slow down, smell, see, and feel what's around you.

Exercise daily. Many times we may make excuses. The biggest one is, "I don't have the time." Stop the excuses. In 24 hours, you don't have the time to take care of yourself? Re-evaluate your life and stop making excuses! The dishes, laundry, and floors can wait, and by doing so you will be a better mother, father, sister, or brother.

Beauty is everywhere! While many of us are so blinded by what we need to get done, we ignore it as it stands in front of us. We are so blessed, but because we are so busy doing other things, we miss it. Please take the time to breathe, look around, find gratitude, and never take anything for granted.

☼☼☼

When life gets too hard to stand, kneel and pray.

-Anonymous

Tradition

If anyone has ever seen the musical *Fiddler on the Roof*, one of the songs is about tradition. A tradition is a customary and cultural practice and there are many in Italy, such as the Bruschetta and Lily Festivals, the Roman Catholic Church's religious festivals, art and culture, and even the practice of eating foods such as olive oil, olives, tomatoes and mozzarella for breakfast. Traditions are important. They give us a sense of belonging and purpose. Make your own traditions for you and your loved ones.

St. Peter's Basilica – Roma, San Pietro Basilica

U
Ultra

Ultra-size your life, not your food!

Italian people eat in moderation. American people eat in excess. But I am not taking about food, I am talking about living an extraordinary life by living it to the fullest.

Ultra-size your giving, ultra-size your compassion, ultra-size your love. Do it big, do it in excess, and do it above and beyond.

St. Peter's Square, Rome – Di San Giovanni in Laterano

Altar of the Fatherland, Rome – Roma, Altare Della Patria

V

Vino

Italy has the most amazing vineyards. The beauty of the mountainside is spectacular. The wines are vast in variety. Did you know that wine has antioxidants, resveratrol, flavonoids and polyphenols? The Italians keep wine on the table and enjoy it with meals. Of course, it's suggested to drink in moderation, limited to one glass per day.

Florence

Milan – Castello - Brera

W

Walk

Walking, particularly walking outdoors, allows us an opportunity to become a part of nature. Another way to get an opportunity to walk would be to walk a dog. If you don't have a dog, walk a friend's dog, a neighbor's, a shut-in's, or perhaps an elderly neighbor's. Italy is very pet friendly. Everywhere you go, you see dogs. They are not excluded from any businesses, including cafes. Walking a dog could boost your mood. In Italy, dogs are accustomed to people, as they are equal members of society. Take every opportunity to walk every day.

Pisa

Altar of the Fatherland, Rome, St. Peter's Square, 5 a.m.

XXXXXO

Italians are very affectionate people. Grown men hug each other, and they appear to not be caught up with boundaries. Boundaries are important in the U.S. culture. We teach children to respect boundaries at an early age. Perhaps boundaries are not such a big deal for the Italians as they share supper tables in such small places. In some of the local restaurants they join unfamiliar groups together. In America, we very seldom would be joined or mixed into another group.

I come from a family of huggers and kissers, so it takes a lot for me not to hug my patients when they are in pain. But aside from that, I try to show affection to my loved ones daily. There is a lot of research that shows the healing effects that touch has on the mental health of individuals.

Rio Caronica, Castello

Venice – San Marco

Y

Yoga

Yoga is one modality of exercise which assists with self-care practices. Self-care is essential for survival. These daily practices reduce stress and enhance overall long-term health and well-being. If we don't take care of our self, we will become burned out and get sick. We can learn a lot from the Italian culture and slow down the pace of our lives. By doing so, we achieve a healthier and more rewarding balance in our life.

Basilica of San Francesco d'Assisi

Z

Zuppa

The soup in Italy is amazing, especially in Tuscany. Zuppa is part of the benefits of a well-balanced Mediterranean diet. Start a new tradition in your home, shut off the TV, and put electronic devices away. Mealtime should be a relaxed occasion enjoyed in the great company of family and friends.

About the Author

Jo-Ann Petrucci-Andrews provides counseling for children, adults, adolescents, couples and families, caring for a wide range of behavioral, emotional, cognitive, biological, social, parenting, and family issues. She works with issues associated with anger management, adoption, foster care, autism spectrum disorders, bereavement, developmental disabilities, divorce & co-parenting, and mood disorders. Jo-Ann has worked for a variety of nonprofit community-based programs providing treatment for families and is committed to family, school, and community engagement.

Jo-Ann holds a Doctorate Degree in educational leadership from Johnson and Wales University and has an EBD in the PhD clinical counseling program from Capella University, in Minneapolis. Jo-Ann is also a graduate of Providence College where she earned a master's degree in pastoral counseling and guidance counseling. She completed her undergraduate studies at Rhode Island College where she received her Bachelor of Arts in psychology, and at The University of Steubenville where she earned a Bachelor of Arts in theology.

She is a licensed mental health counselor and has a private practice in Woonsocket and Warwick, Rhode Island.

Jo-Ann is a member of the Association of Rhode Island Authors, and currently lives on New England farm with her husband, children, and animals.

www.ingramcontent.com/pod-product-compliance
Lightning Source LLC
Chambersburg PA
CBHW042258280426
43661CB00097BA/1177